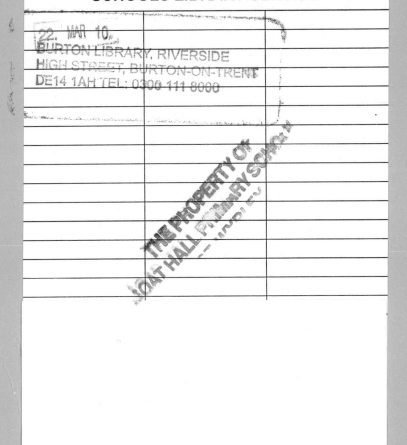

Feelings

Angry

Sarah Medina
Illustrated by Jo Brooker

Raintree

www.raintreepublishers.co.uk
Visit our website to find out more information about **Raintree** books.

To order:
☎ Phone 44 (0) 1865 888112
🖹 Send a fax to 44 (0) 1865 314091
💻 Visit the Raintree Bookshop at **www.raintreepublishers.co.uk** to browse our catalogue and order online.

First published in Great Britain by Raintree, Halley Court, Jordan Hill, Oxford OX2 8EJ, part of Harcourt Education.
Raintree is a registered trademark of Harcourt Education Ltd.

Editorial: Dan Nunn, Cassie Mayer and
   Diyan Leake
Design: Joanna Hinton-Malivoire and
   Ron Kamen
Picture research: Erica Newbery
Illustration: Jo Brooker
Production: Duncan Gilbert

Originated by Modern Age
Printed and bound in China by
   South China Printing Company

ISBN 978 1 4062 0634 0
11 10 09 08 07
10 9 8 7 6 5 4 3 2 1

British Library Cataloguing in Publication Data
Medina, Sarah
Feelings: Angry
152.4'7

A full catalogue record for this book is available from the British Library.

Acknowledgements
The publishers would like to thank the following for permission to reproduce photographs: Bananastock p. **22A, B**; Getty Images/Taxi p. **22C**; Punchstock/Photodisc p. **22D**.

Every effort has been made to contact copyright holders of any material reproduced in this book. Any omissions will be rectified in subsequent printings if notice is given to the publishers.

Contents

Some words are shown in bold, **like this**. They are explained in the glossary on page 23.

What is anger?

Feelings are something you feel inside. Everyone has different feelings all the time. Anger is a feeling.

happy

proud

sad

When you feel angry, you may feel upset. Your face might feel hot. You might want to shout, "It's not fair!"

5

What happens when I am angry?

Anger sometimes makes you want to shout or scream. You may want to hit something. You may burst into tears.

Anger can be a very strong **feeling**.
It can give you a **stomach ache** or
a headache.

Why do I feel angry?

You might feel angry if someone breaks your toy. You might feel angry if someone is mean to you.

8

You might feel angry if you cannot do
something you are trying hard to do.

Is it OK to feel angry?

It is normal to feel angry sometimes.
The important thing is what you do
when you feel angry.

When you are angry, you should not hurt anyone else with what you say or do. Not ever!

What can I do if I am angry?

1, 2, 3, 4 ...

When you feel angry, stay **in control**.
Take a deep breath and count to ten.

If you can, tell someone calmly that you feel angry. Or punch your pillow. You won't hurt it!

Will I always feel angry?

Feelings change all the time. Your angry feelings will not last for ever. You will feel better very soon.

Sometimes, someone else might be angry about something. Remember, they will not stay angry for long, either.

How can I tell if someone is angry?

When someone is angry, they may look red and cross. They might talk loudly or shout at you.

They may not want to play with you
or talk to you. Sometimes, they might
say mean things to you.

Can I help when someone is angry?

You can help people when they are angry. Be nice to them and offer to help them.

Tell them that they can talk to you about why they feel angry. Ask them to play with you!

Is it ever good to feel angry?

Everyone feels angry sometimes.
Anger is OK if it does not hurt you
or anyone else.

It is good to learn what to do with angry **feelings**. Remember, being happy is much more fun!

What are these feelings?

A

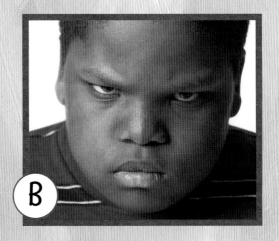

B

C

D

Which of these people look happy?
What are the other people feeling?
Look at page 24 to see the answers.

22

Picture glossary

feeling

something that you feel inside. Anger is a feeling.

in control

when you stay calm, even if you feel angry

stomach ache

when you have a pain in your stomach

Index

Answers to the questions on page 22
The person in picture C looks happy. The other people could be lonely, angry, or sad.

Note to Parents and Teachers
Reading for information is an important part of a child's literacy development. Learning begins with a question about something. Help children think of themselves as investigators and researchers by encouraging their questions about the world around them. Most chapters in this book begin with a question. Read the question together. Look at the pictures. Talk about what you think the answer might be. Then read the text to find out if your predictions were correct. Think of other questions you could ask about the topic, and discuss where you might find the answers. Assist children in using the picture glossary and the index to practice new vocabulary and research skills.

Titles in the *Feelings* series include:

Hardback 978 1 4062 0634 0

Hardback 978 1 4062 0638 8

Hardback 978 1 4062 0635 7

Hardback 978 1 4062 0637 1

Hardback 978 1 4062 0639 5

Hardback 978 1 4062 0636 4

Find out about the other titles from Raintree on our website www.raintreepublishers.co.uk